Mind, Body, & SOL

a poets interpretation of the human experience.

Bella Ruiz

Made with ❤ on the BookLeaf Publishing Platform
www.bookleafpub.in
www.bookleafpub.com

Dedication

To every reflection with whom I am directly connected,
I dedicate this to you.
May you nurture the seeds planted by my words with
love and tender care.

Preface

I recognize I am only one of many beacons through which life directly flows. You, the reader, are another.

We are the personification of the universe, all of whom were granted the gift of experiencing itself.
In simple terms, we are the fingers on the hand of God, Jah, higher source and any other name you may call spirit.
This means embracing the good, the bad, the unknown and the known.
In my understanding, the meaning of life is to live and experience it to its fullest extent, no matter the terms you choose to live it by.
You have the power to define these terms for yourself.

With this book, I set the intention of allowing my writing to be a testament to this awareness. If my poems resonate with you, it is simply because the knowing already exists within you. My word is only a gateway for these knowings to be pulled out of you. Should you find yourself wanting to thank me for this, this is your reminder to thank yourself for being open to receiving first. Thank you for being here with me.
I love you, enjoy.

Acknowledgements

I would like to acknowledge life, to whom I am a direct student. I will always be learning, and I find peace in knowing I will never know it all.
I acknowledge every individual who has supported me in any creative endeavor I choose to pursue. To any who have taken time to hear me speak on a stage and to those who are holding this book now, you are so highly valued.
Your continuous love and support motivates me in more ways than you realize.

To my mother Melissa and my father Alex,
Thank you for allowing me to experiment and express myself in this life. From the time I picked up a violin to me now writing this book, never once have you guys shut down my creative expression. Without the both of you, I could not shine as bright as I am now.

To Professor Arturo Mancha,
The first person to ever hear a poem out of me and the reason I went to my first open mic night.
Your words and life stories ignited a fire in me that grew dim prior to being apart of your English course. Through a dark period in my life, you reminded me of

my light and offered me kind words. For that, I am
eternally grateful.

1. SOL.

I do not claim this name in vain.
Sol is not just an ode to the grandeur of stars,
But a testament to the gentle truth that warmth and light
is a gift not meant to be taken lightly.

In the quiet corners of existence, I seek to shine bright,
a steady presence in the lives that brush alongside my
own.
Like the sun's light that graces the crust of the earth,
I strive to reach beyond myself,
offering warmth in the form of presence,
a quiet illumination to the paths of others.

My light is not blinding but nurturing,
a tender glow that fosters growth in the fertile soil of our
shared experience.
In conversations that ripple with truth,
in gestures of kindness that drift like the sun filtering
through a window at sunrise,
I become a catalyst for change, a gentle force that stirs

the currents of collective evolution.
To radiate is to be a witness to the unfolding journey of
those around me,
And to be a silent encouragement,
a reminder that even in the shadows
you too can shine into the depths of your darkness.

Sol.
I embrace the role of an unassuming and eternally
supportive guide,
and my light a reflection of the broader truth that we all
are interconnected.
Through small acts of illumination,
we contribute to the rise of something greater,
a shared ascent into our highest selves.

____

Sol,
no reclamo este nombre en vano.
Sol no es solo una oda a la grandeza de las estrellas,
sino un testimonio de la suave verdad de que el calor y la
luz son un don que no debe tomarse a la ligera.
En los rincones tranquilos de la existencia, busco brillar
intensamente,
una presencia constante en las vidas que rozan la mía.
Como la luz del sol que acaricia la corteza de la tierra,
me esfuerzo por alcanzar más allá de mí mismo,
ofreciendo calor en forma de presencia,

una iluminación tranquila para los caminos de los demás.
Mi luz no es cegadora sino nutritiva,
un resplandor tierno que fomenta el crecimiento en el
suelo fértil de nuestra experiencia compartida.
En conversaciones que ondulan con verdad,
en gestos de amabilidad que flotan como el sol
filtrándose a través de una ventana al amanecer,
me convierto en un catalizador de cambio, una fuerza
suave que agita las corrientes de la evolución colectiva.
Radiar es ser testigo del viaje que se despliega en quienes
me rodean,
y ser un aliento silencioso,
un recordatorio de que incluso en las sombras
también puedes brillar en las profundidades de tu
oscuridad.
Sol.
Acepto el papel de guía modesto y eternamente solidario,
y mi luz es un reflejo de la verdad más amplia de que
todos estamos interconectados.
A través de pequeños actos de iluminación,
contribuimos al ascenso de algo mayor,
un ascenso compartido hacia nuestros más altos seres.

2. LOVE.

Many have misconstrued loves concept,
Made love into a give and take,
Something to break,
Made to wait on but these textbook definitions could
never define
Love.
I have lost so much & loved even more.
I love so much it oozes from me,
Spilling over the edges like a tub when you forgot you
left the water running,
Love.
I don't believe in falling in love.
I've always felt love makes us rise.
It's tried to disguise itself in others until I realized I was
its source,
Love.
I am in love with everything I see,
In love with all I be,

yes, I am love.

Not the chocolate and floral arrangement type of love
Never the cheap wine and Netflix type of love,
The mind quieting, soul consuming type of love.
The seeing the universe in their every feature type of
love

The discovery of a new favorite song type of love.
Love that gets you out of bed to see the sunrise ona
weekend even though it's 7am type of
love.
The love that pushes you to perfect every family recipe,
Even when you never touched a stove but they gotta
know you can cook.
The recognizing how bright the stars are tonight type of
love,
reminding you some things are too beautiful to be
captured on camera.

Every experience is a gateway to bliss,
No experience is one I miss cause I'm so connected not
attached to
Love.
I can't help but spread this love,
To compliment every woman I see,
Showing her how easy it is to be in love with herself.
Not needing a mans validation,
No time wasted on seeking confirmation that she is

Love.
For the men who always seek it,
Felt he could never reach when he was denied and
pushed away,
Looked at love as a game,
Was shamed into not sharing himself with himself, but
A battle of the sexes cannot stop the force which lies in
Love.
Beyond human connection,
Beyond February 14th,
Or attraction to my gold teeth.
Past the 'can you do this' or having dates you can't miss
cause if you do all hell breaks lose.
A space where heaven is birthed instead,
Love.
A quantum experience,
This magnetic way of being in which you allow yourself
abundance.
When the flood gates open& you swim instead of drown,
and you can't help but pour into another's cup,
Because pouring into yours isn't enough.
Love.
To Love is to Be.
To Be is to Live.
To reflect this truth in life is to be Divine.
As God is, I am love.
& I aim to spread this love,

not because anyone asks,
But because you don't
& I believe you deserve it anyways.

3. I love you like a writer.

My ink-stained hands search for the prints of your
fingers,
trying to catch the essence of you like fireflies in a jar of
words.

Your laughter spills like liquid gold,
each note a spark in the shadowed depths of my page.
I trace its arc, a constellation charted in metaphors.
Your eyes are galaxies I navigate,
swirling with ancient secrets,
a thousand stars caught in the reflection of a moonlit sea.
I seek to map their brilliance with careful lines,
but they shift and shimmer,
slipping through my crafted confines.

Your touch is a storm at sea,
waves crashing on the shore of my solitude,
a tempest I try to enclose within the borders of a stanza.
Each wave I write is an echo,
a whisper of the uncontainable.

You are the dawn breaking through a dark night,
a sunrise painted in the hues of dreams yet to be
revealed.

I pen your arrival with trembling breath,
each word a brushstroke on the canvas of my longing,
but the light of you spills over,
defying the edges of my art.

In my verses, you are a comet,
a streak of brilliance against a canvas of black,
a fleeting blaze that rebels against
the boundaries of my ink.

I catch fragments,
shadows of what I yearn to capture,
but you remain untamed,
wild and infinite.
You, my star,
lie beyond the reach of any penned line.
I write to hold you,
to encase your spirit in the fragile glass of poetic
imagery,
But each attempt is a sigh in the great expanse
of what cannot be fully known or named.

So I keep writing,

with a heart laid bare on each page,
hoping that somewhere in the vastness
of metaphors and verses,
the true essence of you might find its way into the
spaces
between my words and my affection.

4. I love me like a writer.

Within the quiet sanctuary of my being,
I sit and breathe, the world falling away,
to find the canvas of my own existence,
where self-love is both paint and brush.

My body is a vessel of cycles and scars.
I touch my skin, the geography of my journey,
each curve and line a testament to the landscapes
I have traversed, the battles I have won.
I see beauty in the rise and fall of my chest,
in the strength of my limbs that carry me through the
ebb and flow of daily tides.
The way my heartbeat plays a symphony of life,
its pulse a reminder of the vibrant dance
that sustains me.

Within my mind, a garden flourishes,
rich with thought and quiet wisdom.
I honor the chaos and the calm,
the flashes of insight and the shadows of doubt,

each thought a petal in the ever-unfolding flow
of my consciousness, fragrant with possibility.

My soul, a boundless ocean of deep hues,
knows the language of stars and silence.
I embrace the depth of my emotions,
the tides that surge with passion and rest,
the quiet moments that whisper truths
beyond the clamor of the world's demands.

In this space, I am both the artist and the art,
carving out the contours of my self-love
with the precision of a poet's pen.
I see my reflection not as an image to critique,
but as a masterpiece, evolving and true,
an ever-shifting mosaic of joy and growth.

Radical self-love is not a destination
but the journey itself, a path walked with
soft steps and open arms.
I recognize the beauty in my uniqueness,
in the scars that tell stories
and the quiet strength that lies within.
I stand in awe of my own presence,
celebrate the vastness of my being,
and hold myself with tender reverence,
for in loving myself fully,

I discover the boundless beauty of
a soul at home in its own embrace.

13

5. LIBERATION.

Today, I Liberate myself from you.
God how good it feels to say it
and know it's true,
I have liberated myself from you.
I have forgiven you of the pains you inflicted on me,
Which is to say I allow you power over me no longer.
I have cut the cord of attachment,
leaving you no longer latching onto me for energy.
This moment is mine in totality
This moment is mine in totality
This moment is mine in totality
This moment belongs to me.
I am able to see beyond the veil.
I understand now I am meant to prevail and pour all life
force back into my being.
All the time I spent pleasing the version of you that
made me feel safe,
I know now I shouldn't wait on you to love you,
to be able to love me.
You could only give me what you gave yourself after all.

Let me repeat myself,
You can only give to others what you can give to
yourself.
Your capacity to love is tied to your health.
When I look in the mirror I don't see the pain you
caused,
I see the observer of it.
And though she is flawed she is divine,
because her stories are all mine.
I accept every aspect of this life.
Acceptance doesn't mean it is all good,
It means it is, and I allow it to be.
Time no longer has a grip on me.
No I am not perfect, but I am growing.
I hold no fear in showing the process of evolution
May nothing prove to be a pollutant to my spirit.
This is my expression, here & now I wear it.
Now matter how anyone perceives me,
My highest self there is no reason to fight your views,
own them.
Because I know me,
I was never anything to prove.
Today, I liberate myself from you.

6. Love of change.

Change is inevitable.
My brain knows this but my spirit seems to lag behind
sometimes.

It's like I'm trying to get a grip on a reality that doesn't
exist,
While simultaneously striving to emit a new chemical
signature
so that I can create-
what, I don't know.
If I lost that reality I can still move foward,
right?
No not right, left, down, up, diagonal??
f*ck I forgot the steps.

I find myself lost again,
because I can't see the end of this tunnel,
Feel like I'm slipping thru a funnel with no filter at the
end, I want to create
but I don't know where I am.

Can't figure out where I'm standing now so how can I
pick up my dragging feet?
But I've never been one to accept defeat so here I go
crawling into darkness.

Falling down the rabbit hole, I chased the white rabbit
with a ticking clock and now I don't know how to stop
watching time.
Time.
Time can't define what I am.
I don't exist in the past or future,
I am here and I am now.
I flow despite not knowing how I'm meant to move,
So let me not try to manipulate my movement.

I took that lesson from the water.
See the water knows no bodies, it can be
held

but not bound,
Its purpose isn't found in what it rests in but how it
changes.
How the heat makes it weightless and weight makes it
fall,
see I recognize constant change is natural.

I took that lesson from the trees.
Watching the colors of the leaves go from green to
yellow, yellow to brown the
leaves snap off and are left on the ground
But hang on,
we are talking about the trees.
The trees don't breakdown about losing all they know.
They create more when it's time to grow and they tune
into to themselves through it all.
The trees allow the wind to snatch what's not serving
them.
The dead leaves were a burden and they celebrate the
loss.

Impermanence is a paradox that once consumed me,
I'm talking chewed up, spit out, sh*t out,
Drew from me and my living experiences as I
questioned
'How is this going to change??',
Because If I live too long, I'm afraid I'll die.

But, the end is inevitable.
Instead of denial I open my arms to the unknown.
That action alone proves how much I've grown because
in not fearing death,
I live.
I live for the uncertainty,
for the constant shifts in my reality. I don't know what
comes next,
But I accept it already. I embrace my transitions.
To rise in love at the risk of falling out of love.
To live until I die.
To smile and also cry until I can't breathe,
tears till I can't see before I clear my eyes to release,
and breath again.
How could I not be grateful for the inevitability
Of change?

7. Lust of change.

I have to admit,
me and changes love has turned to lust.
Change, you entice me,
whispering promises of the new into my ear,
and my spirit falls under the impression.
You leave me aching for the thrill of uncharted paths,
even if they lead to chaos because somehow,
comfort became a cage.
Its bars invisible but confining
And I, too weary to endure the monotony of sameness.

So I chase the horizon of change,
Sculpting my life with sudden shifts,
Unfamiliar landscapes emerging
From the ruins of old certainties.

"Oh change,you are my muse",
I say.
A relentless tide that swept away
The anchored remnants of yesterday, leaving behind a

mosaic of possibility.

"Guide me into the unknown"
I say,
I don't wanna know where I'm heading.
You innerstand my love of the potential for potential.
Seeking constant movement so as to never become
stagnant,
shifts in my reality,
Losses and regrowth,
death and rebirth.

And so I weave change into my days,
A tapestry of disruption and surprise,
Stirring the dust of routine Into a storm of new
beginnings.
Each shift a rebellion,
Each alteration a plea for motion,
Everything needs to be rearranged.

So I rearrange my room in the middle of the night.
Put my bed by the window so I may rest my head in the
moonlight.
It's not enough.
Cut off dead connections to make way for better.
better comes.
It's not enough.

Got a hair cut, hair colored,
dead weights gone and it's still not enough.
Change, will it ever be enough?
Maybe there's an answer within my question.

In the fragments of renewal, I found a strange solace,
Because in the shadow of relentless change,
I came to discover a rhythm all my own.
In the embrace of constant motion,
I learned to dance with uncertainty without stepping on
their toes.
I find a fierce beauty in the unpredictable,
loving change once again in its purest form,
as a child would.

Change
A liberation in the art of becoming.

8. 20 something.

Our early twenties.
A time when freedom dances just out of reach,
And the world spins with promises of uncharted
territories and boundless joys.
My dreams are as bright as I am,
and every day feels like a chance to grasp the
shimmering edges of
who I am meant to become.

But here, in the press of reality,
I am met with the weight of bills and hidden fees,
the hollow clamor of a system that seems more eager to
exhaust than to inspire.
I am left navigating a landscape littered by student loans
and rent checks,
the mirage of stability flickering against the backdrop of
uncertainty.

The hours are long, and seldom pay enough.
in the quiet moments, It seems

I hear doubts whisper louder than ambitions screams.

My friends, too, carry their burdens,
Each grappling with the same elusive promise as though
success were a distant shore,
forever beyond the reach of the youth.

Yet, in the quiet of midnight, when dreams feel just a
heartbeat away,
there's a spark of defiance— a belief in tomorrow's
possibility.
We are here, in the midst of it, finding our way through
the thicket.
Though the path is rugged and unclear, there is a fierce
strength in our persistence.
It is the glimmer you catch in fleeting moments of
serenity, the reassuring pulse of life's rhythms that
promise change, even in stagnation.

9. Therapist friend.

I am the therapist friend.
You have time to rant to me about your day,
Ask me what I have to say but not enough to ask how
mine was?
How any of mine have been?
Not that I need it but the courtesy is still appreciated,
cause when you don't
It makes me think my advice is valued more than my
company.
And I don't wanna assume anything, but our
conversations have turned to interviews.
The sh*t you say, I see through.
Our friendship is a blur of question & answer,
Even when my tia got cancer I don't recall you saying
anything besides "me&mine".
I let you think I was fine so yes it's on me too, that's
true,
but a healers heart can get cold too.
Always trying to save everyone else,
to balance it with saving yourself is a heavy task.

I don't wanna have to ask my people to be there,
Swear up & down it's all love but,
When life gets me down my spirit offers me a hug since
you've been absent.
This poem is for me to release the past when you
neglected my feelings,
Thought I was healing but something in me still feels
triggered.
Finger on the trigger aiming at this so called friendship,
maybe if I just pull it quick it won't hurt so bad.
I used to get so mad when you would ignore my calls,
So much so my fists curled into balls but,
now I'm breathing.
Now I see I shouldn't be your therapist friend.
So please, get a real therapist,
I'm no longer clocked in.

10. UNTITLED.

I don't wanna pollute this space with words.
Sometimes I just wanna enjoy the silence with you.
Try and tune into the indistinct chatter of the bugs
hiding in the grass.
Or tune into the songs the wind chose to sing today.
Can you hear her melodies?

11. Yes, I can overcome.

Dear reader,
Life doesn't repeat itself, it rhymes.
You may think there was a moment you were at a prime,
maybe you haven't allowed yourself to build up from
now.
Cause how could you say your life is over if you're still
breathing?
Each moment conceiving new opportunities to learn.
Better to allow the past to warm than to burn.
Those lessons were meant to be a guide not a life
sentence.
Moments left for you to reference & say
"yes, I can overcome.",
Yes, you can overcome.
In saying those words you've already won the battles
you've faced,
and those you've yet to make it past but
How can you pass something without growing through?
Movement and motion are often misconstrued cause
You can say you're progressing all you want but,

Let us not put on a front that you've dealt with the one
skeleton in your closet you still fear the most.
Once it's revealed don't go around boasting on the
others who still feel scared.
Be aware that your journey will never be theirs and
that's a blessing.
Even if you failed your testing atleast you have
unlimited attempts.
They're only granted when you take a moment to
glimpse behind the veil of your perceived failures.
And realize that those curtains are actually sails to push
your ship out to sea.
Yes, I can overcome.
Yes, you can overcome.

12. Between the border.

Soy una mujer chicana viviendo en los Estados Unidos.
In the shadows of my two worlds,
I remain torn between the rhythm of Spanish and
cadence of English.
Mis palabras are broken,
my tounge cursing the interactions con mi gente,
Deeming me incomplete as I do not fit the mold of what
it means to be 'Mexican enough'.
In the eyes of my bloodline, I am an outsider,
A misfit caught between the verses
of a language I cannot perfect.

Yet,in the soils I was raised upon
I am branded with the label "dirty Mexican,"
Mi piel morena a gateway to ridicule.
Mi existencia se reduce
to a stereotype, a narrow perception that fails to see the
depth of my dual heritage
due to being blinded by my gold,
though my gold shining bright as my so(u)l.

A place where I witness my people being hunted down,
Criminalized,
denied of their rights to live,
And I question what more I can give besides my vote.

Nowadays Mexican has become synonym to destruction
of a pearly white America that could do no wrong in the
eyes of our oppressors.
Because somehow they win every bloodbath fought.
Atleast that's what I was taught by McGraw-Hill.
No mention of the fears instilled,
Generational curses, promises never fulfilled,
Inheritance of an unjust system that was never built to
build with us.
Susurros de vergüenza sobre tierras robadas,
Prideful celebrations for the American dream.
& The best part about the dream,
you get to stay asleep.
stay asleep.
stay asleep.
stay asleep.
No need to worry about truth when you're caught in
REM.
Even if they awoke, they may defend the dreams they've
come to know.
Which just goes to show the only thing we can control,
Is our state of consciousness.

soy una mujer chicana viviendo en los Estados Unidos.
I've been questioned on my identity, my brown skin,
'Oh she must be Egyptian, maybe Indian',
Pero me conozco. No puedes decirme quién soy.
Soy la sangre que se derramó en nuestros suelos,
las flores que crecieron del concreto.
Soy las canciones que cantan nuestras madres,
las lágrimas que derramaron nuestros ancestros.
I strive not to rewrite history,
But to start again in a new timeline.
A beacon of light & hope,
Because this don country could never dim a light
as bright as my own.
Sol.

13. GEMINI.

I love you,
no I don't.

I hate you,
no I won't say that you just hurt me.

Im sorry, my tounge got a habit of cursing sh*t when I'm
mad but I'm cool now.
My open mind is what allows me to innerstand you.

Oh you think I'm profound boo?
Cause I can create a lot more than poems.
Wanna learn every art form just to show the world that
this girl got
a lot to get out of her system.

Thinking,
thinking,
thinking,
new words always consume my brain.

Sometimes I can't even catch the thought train but,
I'll wait for the next ride.

Will do some other things on the side like
speak to him, them & her about all of their dreams.
Pull some inspiration from the reflections I see and
resort back to the depths of my mind when I get the
chance.

Got a bold way of making my stance but I'm flexible too,
I can recognize truth when it's true.
But If it's not in alignment,
it's deuces to you because I can handle all of me.

I know that I got my duality's but it's not 'two faced'.
More like having many ways of expressing myself.
and if that scares you, go get you a cancer.
Or maybe a Scorpio, they might have your answer.
But me? I got questions for you.
Me?? No, I wanna know who you are.

Oh you said I shine bright as a star?
Thank you, I believe I do too,
and that's not self centered just because I agree with
you.
It's appreciated, but not needed.
I'm my own best friend,

The loudest one clapping anytime that i win and
even when I fail, I use that as fuel.
I might go off into my little spiels, but I'm a gemini.
& That's not an excuse I just want you to understand
me,
Maybe make me your muse.

But take in my words first,
that's the way to my heart
Maybe make the little comments about my art,
you know words of affirmations my love language.
And if you think that's something you can manage then
be my guest,
But be careful not to damage because if you f*ck up
once,
that puts you at a disadvantage.
Im ruled by mercury,
celestial, from another planet
And yea I know some people can't stand it but I'm free
as the air is,
Please, don't try to confine me just share this moment
with me
And then maybe,
maybe,
I'll allow you to see into my Gemini mind.

14. Writers block.

As an artist, how do you move through a block?
How do you learn to walk when you've lost the steps to
crawling?
Maybe my creativity is stalling for a reason bigger than
me.
One that I can't see now but I must trust it's for a reason.
I mean, I change with every season,
who's to say my creative energy doesn't too.
But at its abscence the world goes blue.
The colors on my palette look monotone,
bring to figure out if the picture isright or wrong,
As a human I guess it's natural.
Trying to make something people call powerful but
instead,
Just end up with more pressure.

My art shouldn't prove to be a stressor this is my
therapy.
Do you know how hard it is to share me?
My deepest thoughts, my silent prayers,

Peeling back my every layer, I am scared.
But fear doesn't impair my ability to wear my expression
with pride.
My word, which glides off the tongue producing sounds
of the sweetest symphonies.
My word, pushing a message subliminally for you to
have and hold.
My word is all I have until my body goes cold,
I don't take my gift for granted.
After all, my word is one that was granted from God.
I'm not trying to put on a facade, this is me.
Showing up with all my power.
No, I don't need nobody's flowers,
Just confirmation that you're hearing me.
And if you're not, I pray you still receive my blessings.
Every poem I write contains lessons, but I'm not your
self proclaimed teacher.
Im just a woman with her words,
and I hope it'll reach you.

15. Stop, look, listen.

We walk through life, eyes fixed on the horizon,
heads high and observant to the rising and setting
of the sun moon & stars above.
Very rarely do we take time to acknowledge the life
beneath the soles of our feet.
The lives within concrete and asphalt,
the steady paths holding the weight of our footsteps,
just beneath our line of sight,
life pulses in quiet defiance.

Roots stretch and whisper through the soils, weaving a
secret network,
a hidden orchestra of connection,
stretching to quench their thirst with the wells pulsing
within the earth,
conducting the symphony of evolution.
Cracks in the pavement cradle worlds foreign to the
human mind, where ants march in meticulous patterns.
Their purpose, a choreographed survival.

In the grass, blades sway in gentle rhythms, dancing
with the wind in a quiet protest against the
indifferent march of progress,
nourished by the hidden rain, and warmed by the
murmured sun.

The foundations we reside on are not merely a stage for
our journeys, but a canvas of existence;
ever-present, awaiting recognition, awaiting reverence.
Each step upon the earth's surface disturbs a world rich
with hidden wonder, a reminder that the life we tread
upon is a testament to being.

Today, my gaze wandered, not just on the horizon, but to
the life below.
With the shift in perspective, I saw the tapestry woven
in silence beneath my steps.
Here, the hidden thrives, the subtle thrives, awaiting
acknowledgment, or perhaps not seeking
acknowledgment at all.
Not knowing what it is to be acknowledged.
And I, the observer
gain a respect for the ground that carries us,
unacknowleged, unseen,
And forever thriving.

16. PRAYER.

Dear god,

I know there are forces unseen but often it seems I'm just

speaking into the abyss.

But if I don't speak,

I might miss my chance for some miracle to fall into my

lap.

In the Bible it seems you always have my back but when

I cried my eyes remained stained with tears.

My fears that clinged to me all these years,

God why have I not heard from you?

When I meditate I open my self to receiving.

While I lay and focus on my breathing

Ive come to realize that you are not a genie.

I used to despise the idea of faith,

The way I was told I had to wait to know your existence

was more than the stories.

But here & now I recognize your glory,

God,

You are always working in my favor.

For the times I was looking for my savior,
Love was always there.
When I asked you to help me be patient,
I didn't mean send me sh*t to test my patience but,
Once I got thru I recognized the truth that you
Were only allowing me an opportunity to prove to
myself that
I am exactly who I know I am.
I am being all I know I am becoming.
I am seeing just how far love takes me and God
Thank you.
For not being a genie,
but allowing me to be a student and a teacher.
Thru your presence I am able to reach the
Mind body & spirit of all I meet,
With your love I no longer retreat into my old ways.
I am free, today and always.
God, thank you for listening.
ASE

17. CELESTIAL.

I observed the sky today,
and witnessed a labyrinth of tangled lines strangle sky's
breath.
Street lamps burn their artificial stars into her depth,
casting shadows that wrestle with the starlight and
suffocate the midnight blue.
The city's veins pulse with electric whispers,
each wire a thread binding me to this grid.
An intricate web where sky's vast promise is reduced to
a patch of mottled gray.
I yearn for the unfiltered view of night,
for a horizon unmarked by neon scars,
Where the celestial dome is not marred by the flicker of
synthetic balls of fire.
I feel the pull of the open expanse, as an alien would to
their mothership.

I am plagued by an urgent need to sever these
connections,
to cast off the digital shackles and reclaim the uncharted

infinity above.
In the distance,
beyond the clamor of circuitry,
there's a world untouched by the grid's overbearing
presence.
Here, sky is boundless and free.
She is a canvas untraced, awaiting a soul ready to escape
the wires.
And I, the celestial,
anticipate sky's embrace.

18. CREATIVITY.

Creativity is the beating heart of the human condition.

A translation of the soul,
For a language which can only be experienced.
To be an artist is to breathe life into a void.
& to birth visions out of potential,
nurturing them with tranquility & care.
To create is to reside in our natural state of being,
while simultaneously honoring
the essence of humanity.
In this way,
I allow my creative visions to be a testament to this
sacred awareness.

19. Spoken word artist.

I don't usually like labels but I recognize I am a poet.
I don't have to seek beauty, I show it with my twisted
metaphors,
Put so much writing on my headboard as a child I got in
trouble for it.
But those words were a glimpse of what would soon be
of my art.
I don't remember at what point it started.
Maybe my love for books as a child,
Or cramming in extra pages while writing short stories
for my English class.
And yea I passed with flying colors plus my teachers
telling one another I had a gift that must be shared.
Then I got older & my voice was impaired by the eyes on
lookers who often stared without a reaction.
But my words value isn't based on your reactions
I own my voice. My creative expression.
Even when my coworkers told me I should lessen the
impact of the harsh truths I was feeding to their ears,
Though my word wasn't something they wanted to hear

it must be said.

I decided not to let others opinions dictate how bright I
shine,
This page I write on is all mine to pour my soul into,
If only you knew how much I care for you
Just for being alive
And I allow my words to paint vivid images as to why.

20. POET.

Definition?
Someone who writes poems.
-google
a person possesing special powers of imagination or
expression.
-the dictionary
A person capable of breathing life into the lifeless,
Granting a translated expression of the mundane
-Sol

I knew I loved poetry from the moment I looked life and
death in the eyes in one sitting
from a woman I seen hold a mic.
A woman who poured her life force into her words and
knew she deserved every ounce of our attention.
How someone could be so unapologetic in their self
expression,
how they can question and answer living with lessons.
You'd think she was demanding life,
before she began bargaining with death while having a

deep innerstanding of both,
allowing them to peacefully coincide.

Her gaze was distant, but the stories were close,
like a whisper from the edge of night.
Tales of beginnings that folded into endings,
of breaths held and released,
of moments stretched into eternity.
Her words traced the contours of mortality, shaping the
void between birth and oblivion into something beautiful
,
painting a canvas where grief and joy danced in the
shadow of the universe.
With each line, I felt a heartbeat that was not my own,
but shared,
a resonance that hummed in the hollow spaces of my
soul, awakening a love for this strange alchemy.

In that moment, surrounded by the weight of unspoken
truths and the gravity of existence, I discovered a new
language,
Birthed from an old one
one that was a testament to the depth of being, the
fragility of moments, and the endless beauty in the
interfolds of life and death.
The world of poetry became a mirror, reflecting not just
what is, but what might be,

and the rich, tangled layers of human experience that
bridge the moments unfurling between now and eternity.

Poets capture fleeting moments and distilled emotions,
crafting verses that resonate with the echoes of the
human condition.
Through their words, they map the depths of
existence, exploring the spaces where the heart and mind
converge,
and invite readers to journey through the landscapes of
imagination and introspection.

POET

Definition?

*-A weaver of dreams and a seeker of truth, an alchemist
of language who breathes life into silence and transforms
the mundane into the sublime.*

21. Statement piece.

My existence is my statement piece.
My word echoes in the mind of those I encounter,
My light radiates like the sun in spaces I enter,
May my warmth be an aid to your healing self.
The self your highest self is attempting to reach.
I see the potential in each individual.
Your individuality is what makes you beautiful.
Your voice is yours and only yours,
Don't allow anyone else's ideologies to taint your
tounge.
You are the creator of your reality.
You are the master of your mind,
Don't be mastered by the mind.
Don't be a slave to your timeline.
It doesn't matter what he/she did & when they did it,
You are fully capable.
Don't allow others successes to boost your self doubts.
You got your entire life to spend with yourself,
So start living now.
Die to the past every moment, you don't need it.

Only use it when it is absolutely relevant to the now.
Your existence is your statement piece.

51